MW00805706

Suzuki

CELLO SCHOOL

Volume 3
Cello Part
International Edition

AMPV: 1.01

© Copyright 2018, 1992, 1980 International Suzuki Association
Sole publisher for the entire world except Japan:
Summy-Birchard, Inc.
Exclusive print rights administered by Alfred Music
All rights reserved. Printed in USA.

Available in the following formats: Book (0483S), Book & CD Kit (40703)

Book
ISBN-10: 0-87487-483-1
ISBN-13: 978-0-87487-483-9

Book & CD Kit
ISBN-10: 0-7390-9711-3
ISBN-13: 978-0-7390-9711-3

The Suzuki name, alone and in combination with "Method" or "Method International", International Suzuki Association, and the Wheel device logos are trademarks (TM) or Registered Trademarks of the International Suzuki Association, used under exclusive license by Alfred Music.

Any duplication, adaptation or arrangement of the compositions contained in this collection requires the written consent of the Publisher.
No part of this book may be photocopied or reproduced in any way without permission.
Unauthorized uses are an infringement of the U.S. Copyright Act and are punishable by law.

INTRODUCTION

FOR THE STUDENT: This material is part of the worldwide Suzuki Method® of teaching. The companion recording should be used along with this publication. A piano accompaniment book is also available for this material.

FOR THE TEACHER: In order to be an effective Suzuki teacher, ongoing education is encouraged. Each regional Suzuki association provides teacher development for its membership via conferences, institutes, short-term and long-term programs. In order to remain current, you are encouraged to become a member of your regional Suzuki association, and if not already included, the International Suzuki Association.

FOR THE PARENT: Credentials are essential for any teacher you choose. We recommend you ask your teacher for his or her credentials, especially those relating to training in the Suzuki Method®. The Suzuki Method® experience should foster a positive relationship among the teacher, parent and child. Choosing the right teacher is of the utmost importance.

To obtain more information about the Suzuki Association in your region, please contact:

International Suzuki Association
www.internationalsuzuki.org

Under the guidance of Dr. Suzuki since 1978, the editing of the Suzuki Cello School is a continuing cooperative effort of the Cello Committees from Talent Education Japan, the European Suzuki Association and the Suzuki Association of the Americas.

CONTENTS

* Piano accompaniments begin on track 11.

The Four Main Points for Study

1. Have the children listen daily to the records of the music they are studying. This listening helps them to make rapid progress.
2. Tonalization is included in each lesson and is a part of the daily practice at home.
3. Have the children play the second, third, and fourth position with accurate changes and intonation.
4. In Vol. III attention should be paid to ends of phrases.

Tonalization

Each lesson begins with tonalization. Tonalization is stressed in order to improve and refine the tone. During the lesson use both bowing alternatives (down ⊓ and up V) for beginning each exercise.

1 Berceuse

F. Schubert

3rd Position Tonalization

Moon Over The Ruined Castle

R. Taki

At first, practice in 1st position; later, practice in 3rd position.

D Minor Scale Patterns

2 Gavotte

J. B. Lully

Backward Extension

Forward Extension

Open hand between 1st and 2nd fingers by moving thumb, 2nd, 3rd and 4th fingers
one half-step away from the 1st finger. Keep the same shape in the moving fingers.

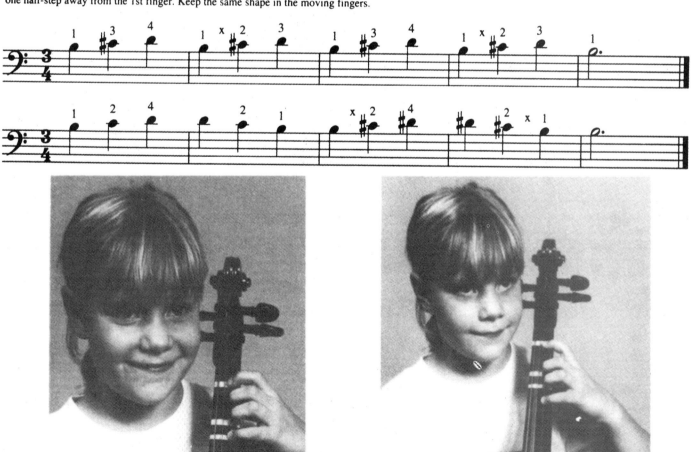

3 Minuet

Moderato e grazioso

L. Boccherini

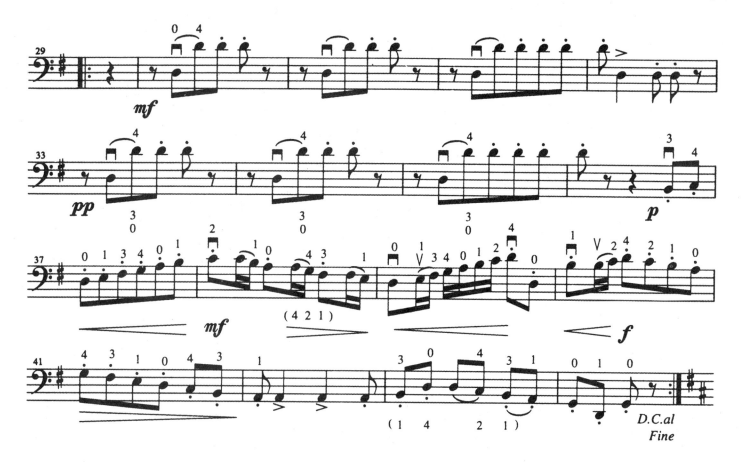

4th Position Tonalization

Moon Over The Ruined Castle

R. Taki

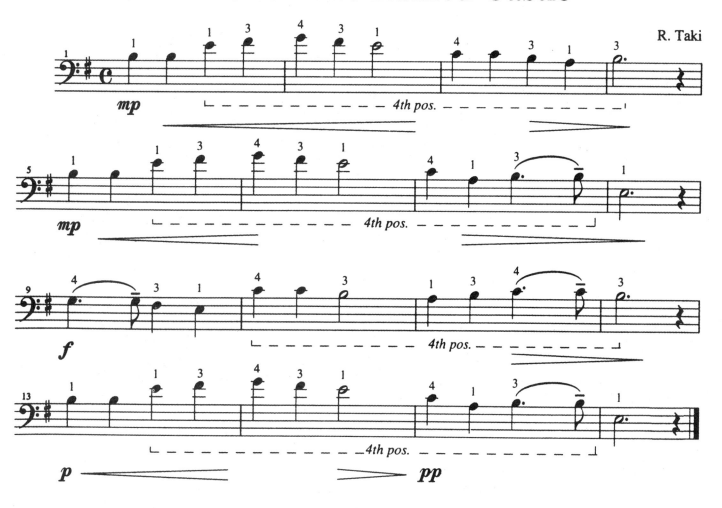

4 Scherzo

C. Webster

* Place only the 4th finger lightly on the A or D string to sound the harmonics.

Half position Exercise

D string

Repeat each exercise on the A string.

5 Minuet in G

L. van Beethoven

At first change position slowly and accurately,
then practice with increasing speed.

Melodic C Minor Scale

Natural C Minor Scale

6 Gavotte in C Minor

Andante

J.S. Bach

7 Minuet No. 3

J. S. Bach

8 Humoresque

A. Dvořák

Poco lento e grazioso

Preliminary practice 1

Use a very short bow stroke. Keep the bow on the string during the rest.

Preliminary practice 2

Stop bow and prepare.
1st finger glides to harmonic A.

Do not release 1st finger.　Slide 3d finger to E and then release.

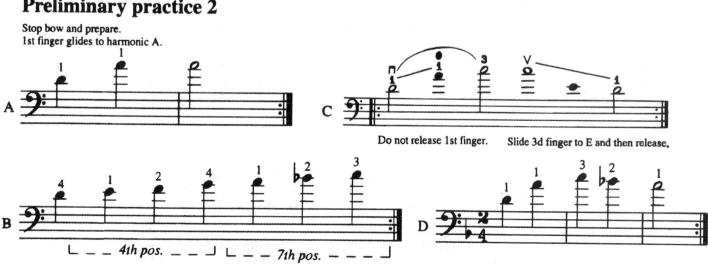

9 La Cinquantaine

(Air in the olden style)

G. Marie (1852-1928)

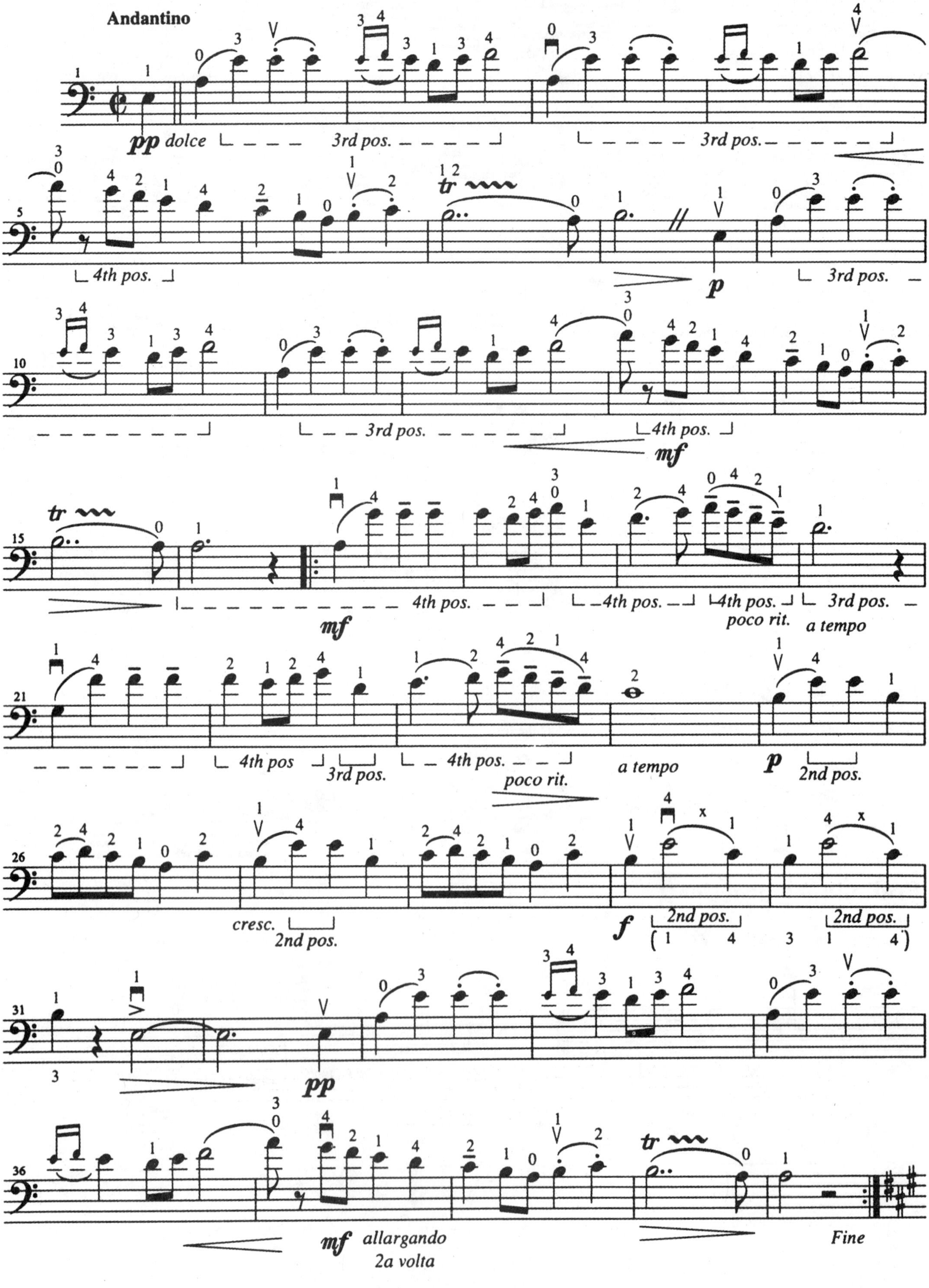

D.C. al Fine

10 Allegro Moderato

J. S. Bach

Position Etudes

3rd Position

A String

D String

* Practice the same on the G and C strings.

4th Position

A String

D String

5th Position

A String

Practice the same on the other strings.

Figure of the 4th position

Major and Minor Scales

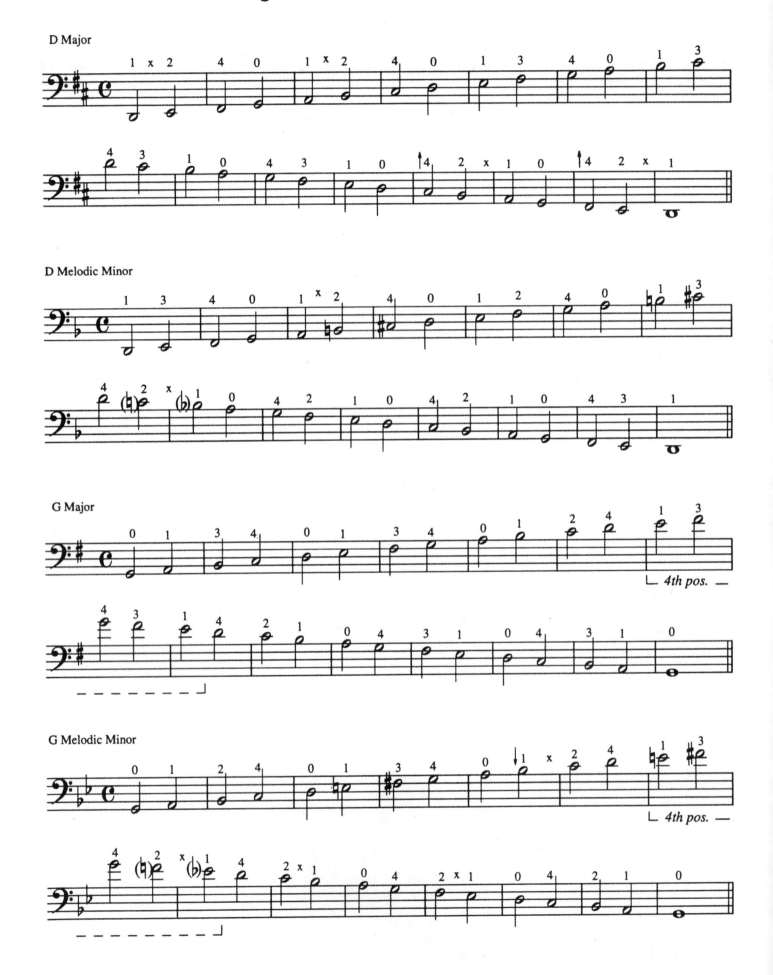

C Major

C Melodic Minor

A Major

A Melodic Minor

Trill Drills

Each group should be clear and even

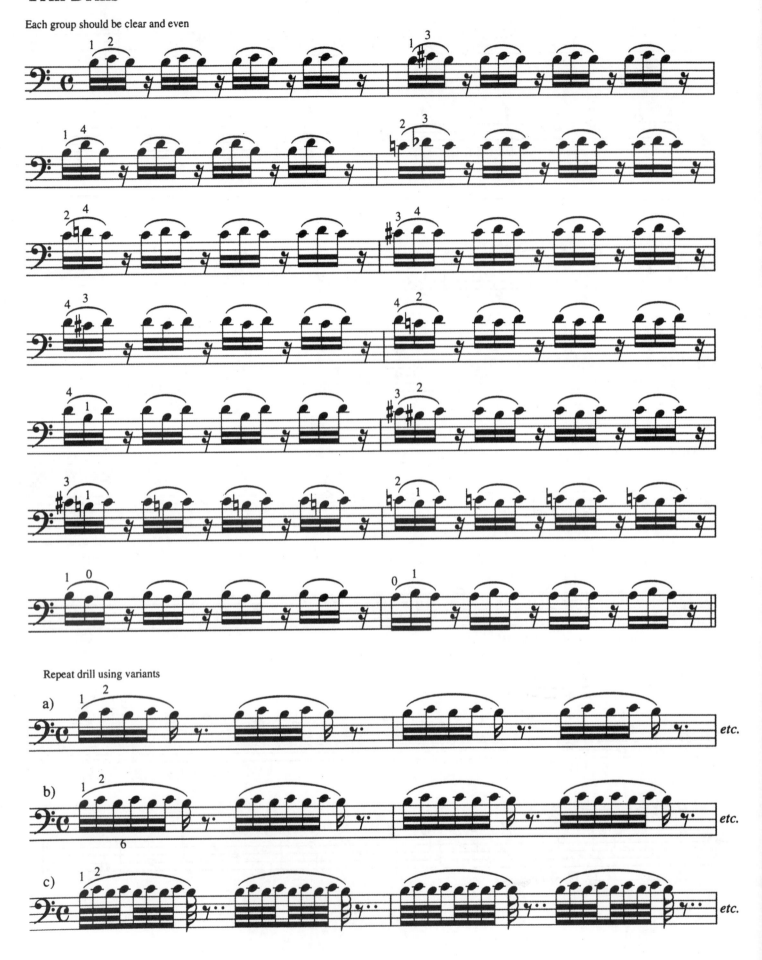

Repeat drill using variants

a)

b)

c)